Jesus: Dead or Alive?

John Blanchard

EP Books (Evangelical Press), Registered Office: 140
Coniscliffe Road, Darlington, Co Durham DL3 7RT
admin@epbooks.org
www.epbooks.org

EP Books are distributed in the USA by: JPL Books,
3883 Linden Ave. S.E., Wyoming, MI 49548
order@jplbooks.com
www.jplbooks.com

First published 2009
This edition 2016

ISBN 978-1-78397-180-0

Jesus: Dead or Alive?

Some time ago I was having a long conversation with an atheist at the University of Cape Town when I was called away to another engagement. Before leaving I asked him one last question: 'What do you think of Jesus Christ?' Without a moment's hesitation he replied, 'I am not sure, but I do know this: everything depends on whether or not he rose from the dead.'

Although he denied the very existence of God, let alone the Bible's claim that Jesus was God in human flesh and form, he was certain that all questions about the identity, ministry and relevance of Jesus hinged on another one: *after he had been executed, certified dead, then buried, did he come back to life?* I could not stay to ask the student how he had come to that conclusion but he was absolutely right — and his 'everything' covers more than he may have realized.

To begin with, the integrity and reliability of the entire New Testament hinge on whether Jesus rose from the dead, because time and again it says that he did. The writers of over ninety-five per cent of the New Testament refer to it often, never once as a myth, legend or theory but always as a historical event. One of them was a physician called Luke, described by Sir William Ramsay, an original member of the British Academy, as one of the very greatest of historians. In one of his two New Testament books Luke writes, *I myself have carefully investigated everything from the beginning* (Luke 1:3, NIV) and in the other he speaks of

3

many convincing proofs (Acts 1:3, NIV) that Jesus came back from the dead. If Jesus did no such thing, not only was this expert witness mistaken, but the New Testament, which so often repeats the claim, is of no more historical value than a fairy tale.

Secondly, if Jesus did not come back to life, he was either a fool or a deluded liar, because he never predicted his death without claiming that he would rise again. For someone to say he was going to die would be to state the obvious, but if he claimed that after being dead and buried he would come back to life we would feel he was in need of a good psychiatrist. Yet Jesus not only repeatedly told his followers he would rise again, he even pinpointed how long after his burial this would happen. Even his enemies reported him as saying, *After three days I will rise* (Matthew 27:63) and as we will see later, they persuaded the authorities to take strict security measures to seal his tomb in case his followers stole the body and faked his resurrection. What is more, dismissing Jesus as a fool or a liar clashes with all the records of his life, which reflect his outstanding integrity, goodness, wisdom and mental balance. Even the British author H. G. Wells, a self-confessed 'unbeliever', was to admit that in judging a person's greatness by historical standards, *Jesus stands first.*

But *did* he come back to life after being dead and buried? The best way to begin answering the question is to take a straightforward look at the background to the resurrection story, the Bible's record of the death and burial of Jesus.

4

The record

Although there was not a shred of evidence to back up his accusers' claims, Jesus was charged with a series of crimes ranging from insurrection to blasphemy. After several hearings he was brought before Pontius Pilate, the Roman governor of Judea, who authorized his crucifixion. Having mocked and flogged him, the Roman soldiers marched Jesus to a place called Golgotha on the outskirts of Jerusalem, where they crucified him. Crucifixion was a barbaric method of execution forbidden by Jewish law but practised by Romans and others, their victims sometimes hanging on a cross for days before dying. Soon after he died, Jesus was buried nearby. The next day, Jewish religious leaders reminded Pilate that Jesus had prophesied that he would rise from the dead in three days. To prevent his followers from removing the body, then claiming that Jesus had come back to life, they asked Pilate to provide special security at the tomb. Pilate agreed and ordered a detachment of soldiers to make the tomb *as secure as you can* (Matthew 27:65). A huge rock had already been placed over the entrance to the tomb and this was now secured with the governor's seal. A round-the-clock guard was posted to ensure that nobody could tamper with the tomb or its contents.

Jesus died at about 3.00pm on a Friday and his devout Jewish followers would have made sure that he was buried before 6.00pm, when the Jewish Sabbath began. On the Sunday morning, the day after the Sabbath, three women (two called Mary and the other called Salome) went to the tomb. When they arrived there was no guard, the seal was broken and the rock had been moved. Understandably, they were terrified; but suddenly an angel appeared and said, *Do not be afraid, for I know that you seek Jesus who was crucified. He is not here, for he has risen, as he said. Come, see the place where he lay. Then go quickly and tell his disciples that he has risen from the dead* (Matthew 28:5-7). On their way back into the city Jesus appeared to them and said, *Do not be afraid; go and tell my brothers to go to Galilee, and there they will see me* (Matthew 28:10).

The missing person

Whatever we think of these incidents there is one fact over which there can be no argument: *by Sunday morning the body had gone*. At least five people who visited the tomb that day (two other followers went to the site after the women) confirmed this. There is no record of anybody denying the fact at the time and 2,000 years later nobody has produced a shred of credible evidence to show that this was not the case.

On the other hand, there was soon a compelling reason for believing that these witnesses were telling the truth. Within a few weeks, Jesus' followers took to the streets, risking their lives by preaching that he had risen. Yet if the tomb was not empty, all the authorities had to do to prove the preachers wrong was to invite people to go there and see the body for themselves. As the German theologian Paul Althaus says, preaching the resurrection of Jesus *could not have been*

maintained in Jerusalem for a single day, for a single hour,
if the emptiness of the tomb had not been established as a
fact for all concerned.

The empty tomb does not prove that Jesus rose from the dead, but to believe that the disciples would risk their own lives by preaching that he was alive when his body lay a few hundred yards away is ridiculous. The empty grave is at the very least an important piece of circumstantial evidence — which not even his enemies could deny.

The Bible's account is clear, but did Jesus come back to life? There are at least two popular approaches to the issue.

Head in the sand

One approach is to ignore the question altogether. At the time of writing, Richard Dawkins, the one-time Charles Simonyi Professor of the Public Understanding of Science at Oxford University, is one of the best-known atheists in the world. In several of his earlier books he included attacks against those who believe in God, but in *The God Delusion,* first published in 2006, he launched a nuclear assault on all religious faiths, with one goal in mind: *If this book works as I intend, religious readers who open it will be atheists when they put it down.*

Early on he states, *I am not attacking any particular version of God. I am attacking God, all gods, anything and everything supernatural,* though one page later he narrows his target: *Unless otherwise stated, I shall have Christianity mostly in mind.* Then he gets even more specific: there is *no evidence* in favour of God's existence; the Bible is a *chaotically cobbled-together anthology of disjointed documents*; *the only difference between* The Da Vinci Code *and the gospels is that the gospels are ancient fiction while* The Da Vinci Code *is modern fiction*; and the central doctrine of Christianity is *barking mad, as well as viciously unpleasant.* As for Jesus, he *probably existed*, but the idea that he came back to life after being dead and buried is *absurd.* This leaves no doubt where Dawkins stands, but as the resurrection of Jesus is directly related to the integrity of the New Testament, the credibility of the Bible as a whole, and even the existence of the God it reveals, we would expect Dawkins to concentrate his closest arguments on his own question: *Did he himself come alive again, three days after being crucified?* Having pinpointed the critical issue, what amount of space does he then give to addressing it? How much time does he spend in assessing the evidence? What proof does he produce to show that it never happened? One word answers all three questions: *None!*

This is surely amazing! To dismiss the resurrection of Jesus as 'absurd' is one thing, but to do so by ignoring it is even more ludicrous. The British author Andrew Wilson hits the nail on the head. In *Deluded by Dawkins?* he says that to make fun of some people's arguments for God but to ignore the resurrection, and then think that by doing so one has removed the basis for belief in God *is to chase the mice out of the sitting-*

room, and ... announce that the house is free of animals, while there is an elephant grinning on the sofa.

Dawkins relishes attacking what Christians believe. I once heard him describe people who accept the universe's creation by God as *yapping terriers of ignorance* and in the *Daily Telegraph* he called a biblical belief system *ignominious, contemptible and retarded.* Yet although he spends nearly 400 pages in *The God Delusion* on a withering attack against God and especially against the Christian faith, he barely mentions the resurrection of Jesus and never once engages with the evidence. To spend the best part of fifteen pages discussing sexual ethics (admittedly an important issue) yet not take even fifteen words to tackle the issue on which the whole of Christianity stands or falls is baffling. Whatever the reason for his silence on the subject, ignoring the resurrection of Jesus is not a sensible option and the many others who do the same are making a similar mistake.

The matter of miracles

Another popular approach is to say that Jesus never came back from the dead, as this would be a miracle and 'miracles don't happen'. The eighteenth-century sceptic David Hume took this line. He said that even if all credible historians agreed that on 1 January 1600 Queen Elizabeth died and was buried, but a month later reappeared, resumed the throne, and ruled England for another three years, he would not believe it; he would assume there must be some other explanation. He once said that the only true miracle was that anybody should believe in them! This is a clever sound bite, but is it correct? *The Chambers Dictionary* describes a miracle as 'an event or act which breaks a law of nature' and for many people this ends the argument; there is nothing beyond the laws of nature, and as the resurrection of Jesus would have involved a miracle it clearly never happened.

If this is so, not only is the resurrection of Jesus ruled out, but the entire Bible self-destructs, because it records well over 200 miracles. Yet this approach makes no sense, because it decides the case before examining it. Any honest assessment of an alleged miracle should begin not by rejecting it out of hand, but by looking into the evidence. If this points to a miracle it demands an explanation beyond the normal laws of nature; refusing to consider this is neither sensible nor honest.

The fact is that *the laws of nature cannot cause anything to happen*. They merely reflect our assessment of how things normally happen. The person who believes in God goes further and says they describe *what God normally causes to happen.* If God exists, and determines the laws of nature, he can override or alter them whenever he chooses, and if he created the entire universe and governs all the laws by which it operates, bringing a dead person back to life would hardly be a problem for him.

This lies behind a statement made by thirteen prominent scientists, most of them university professors, in a letter to *The Times* in 1984: *It is not logically valid to use science as an argument against miracles.* **To believe that miracles cannot happen is as much an act of faith as to believe that they can happen.** *It is important to affirm that science (based as it is on the observance of precedents)* **can have nothing to say on the subject** (emphasis added). Rejecting the resurrection of Jesus because it would have meant a miracle makes no scientific sense. Miracles are not *against* nature, they are *above* nature and to deny their possibility is ignorance masquerading as intelligence. The right approach to any proposed miracle is to set aside all our prejudices and to ask the straightforward, open-minded question, 'Did it happen?' In the case of the resurrection of Jesus, several interesting alternatives have been put forward.

NDE?

There has always been fascinated interest in what have become known as near-death experiences (NDEs) and some people have supposed that this is what took place in the case of Jesus. Early in the eighteenth century, theologian Heinrich Paulus suggested that Jesus fell into a coma on the cross and later, in the cool of the tomb, revived sufficiently to make his way out and then deceive the disciples that he had come back from the dead. Some time later another theologian, Karl Friedrich Bahrdt, claimed that Jesus pretended to be dead, using drugs supplied by the physician Luke, but was later resuscitated by one of his followers. Also in the eighteenth century, yet another theologian, Karl Venturini, put forward the idea that a group of supporters, members with Jesus of a secret society, went to the tomb dressed in white, heard Jesus groaning inside, scared the guards away, then rescued their friend. These are variations of the so-called Swoon Theory, but the physical ordeals that Jesus endured in the hours before his burial are sufficient to rule it out.

Firstly, Pilate had Jesus beaten and 'scourged' (Matthew 27:26). The scourge was a short whip with several leather strips loaded with pieces of metal or glass, or small metal balls. The victim was tied in a bent position, exposing his back to the maximum effect, while the lashes rained on him. The punishment was so vicious that it tore chunks out of his body. Sometimes the victim's back muscles would be so badly shredded that the underlying bones were exposed. The scourge could even whip around to the front of the victim's head and tear out his eyes. Some victims were literally scourged to death.

In the case of Jesus the loss of blood was made worse by 'a crown of thorns' (Matthew 27:29) being jammed on his head before he was led away to crucifixion. Exact details of crucifixion vary, but essentially the victim was stripped naked and his wrists or hands nailed to a cross-beam which was then secured to an upright pole in the ground. The victim's feet were then nailed to the pole and he was left there to die of a combination of shock, blood loss and dehydration.

Two criminals were crucified at the same time as Jesus. As the Jews did not want bodies left hanging during the Sabbath, they asked Pilate to have the victims' legs broken (the usual coup de grâce) to ensure that they were dead; then their bodies could be taken down. Pilate gave permission for this to be done and the legs of the other two men were broken. When the soldiers came to Jesus they *saw that he was already dead* (John 19:33), yet to be absolutely sure one of them rammed a spear into his side, producing a flow of 'blood and water' (John 19:34).

Medical experts give two possible explanations for this description. When a person's heart stops beating, the blood inside the heart chambers clots fairly quickly, then separates into plasma and red blood cells. If the soldier stabbed Jesus near the heart and lungs the spear wound would have produced these two fluids, which a layman might well describe as 'blood and water'.

The second explanation points out that the horrific trauma Jesus suffered before and during crucifixion would almost certainly have caused a build-up of fluid in the pericardial sac surrounding the heart, as well as enlarging the heart chambers with blood. A spear piercing these organs shortly after death, before the blood congealed, would have produced a flow of 'blood and water'.

Whatever the exact medical explanation, John's words ring true — and soon there was further confirmation that Jesus was dead. That evening

Joseph, a wealthy follower of Jesus, went to Pilate and asked permission to remove the body for burial. The Bible records what happened: *Pilate was surprised to hear that he should have already died. And summoning the centurion, he asked him whether he was already dead. And when he learned from the centurion that he was dead, he granted the corpse to Joseph* (Mark 15:44-45). Pilate was not prepared to take Joseph's word that Jesus was dead. Only when this was confirmed by the commanding officer in charge of the execution did Pilate agree to release the body. Wrapping it in linen, Joseph placed the body in the unused tomb he had reserved for his own burial and which was carved out of rock in a nearby garden. At least two women, both called Mary, saw the burial take place.

Then what does even the simplest of the swoon theories ask us to believe? Exhausted, traumatized, and haemorrhaging an immense amount of blood, Jesus lost consciousness while hanging on the cross for six hours, but remained alive, even after his side had been ripped open by the soldier's spear. Then, throughout the entire process of taking his body down from the cross, carrying it to the garden, wrapping it in grave-clothes and laying it in the tomb, nobody noticed the slightest suggestion that Jesus was still breathing.

A stone-cold tomb was hardly an intensive care unit, yet at some time during the following thirty-six hours Jesus came out of a coma and, like some first-century Houdini, wriggled out of a tightly wound shroud layered with a sticky mixture of myrrh and aloes 'about seventy-five pounds in weight' (John 19:39). He then pushed aside the massive rock blocking the entrance to the tomb, breaking the governor's seal in the process, overpowered all the Roman soldiers guarding the tomb and made his way into the city — presumably naked as the linen wrapping was left behind. By the time he met his disciples he had made an astonishing recovery. He persuaded them not that he had returned from the brink of death and was in desperate need of medical attention, but that he had conquered death and broken through into a radiant new dimension of life.

Quite apart from all the other difficulties that a swoon theory faces, the last sentence of our reconstruction would be enough to reject it out of hand. It would mean that after a lifetime in which he was 'without sin' (Hebrews 4:15), Jesus deliberately hoodwinked his closest friends into believing a monstrous lie, knowing that if they believed him they would be ruthlessly persecuted and eventually hounded to death.

There have been more conspiracy theories about the resurrection of Jesus than about the assassination of the American President John F. Kennedy in Dallas, Texas, on 22 November 1963. Some of the Kennedy theories have a measure of credibility; the swoon theories have none.

Poor lighting?

In 1907 the British scholar Kirsopp Lake came up with another ingenious suggestion. Unlike the advocates of the swoon theory, he accepted that Jesus died and was buried as the record says. The Bible tells us that on that first Sunday morning three women went to the tomb to complete the embalming of the body 'at early dawn' (Luke 24:1), but on reading this, Lake had a novel idea: emotionally disturbed and in poor light, the women lost their way and went to the wrong tomb.

At first glance this seems possible, but the idea falls apart as soon as we give it a moment's thought. It is one thing to suppose that three distraught women took a wrong turning in poor light, but this would not account for what happened later. When they went back into the city and told the disciples, Peter and John ran to the tomb to see for themselves. Did they also go to the wrong tomb — in broad daylight? Later, one of the Marys returned. Did she get it wrong again? The other women also returned later. Did they repeat their earlier mistake? What is more, rumours of a resurrection would have spread like wildfire; are we really to believe that on that Sunday morning people were scurrying all over the cemetery looking for one open grave, and that none of them could find the right one? One other thing: *why did nobody ask Joseph, the owner of the tomb?* Is it conceivable that he would carefully choose his own private burial place, lay a dear friend's body in it, then forget where it was? Even if this were so, the Jewish authorities who had hounded Jesus to death would have been more than happy to point people in the right direction.

Apparently brushing all of this aside, Kirsopp Lake then plays fast and loose with the biblical record, which tells us that the women were met by an angel. With no evidence whatever, Lake says it was not an angel but a cemetery caretaker who told the women, 'You are looking for Jesus of Nazareth. He is not here.' This would fit the 'wrong tomb' idea, but Lake omits the crucial words the Bible adds: *He has risen.* His theory is based on attributing the first part of the angel's statement to a caretaker, *then deliberately leaving out the rest.* He changes the meaning of the message, but only by dishonestly tampering with the text.

Another issue helps to destroy Lake's myth. Two of the women had been present at the burial of Jesus just thirty-six hours earlier and 'saw where he was laid' (Mark 15:47). The word translated 'saw' here refers to a person who looks 'with interest and for a purpose, usually indicating the careful observation of details'. Bearing that in mind, would both Marys have forgotten where they had looked so carefully?

Lake tries to counter this: It is very doubtful if they were close to the tomb at the moment of burial ... It is likely that they were watching at a distance. Yet once again he is clutching at straws, as the Bible carefully adds the words that the women 'saw the tomb *and how his body was laid*' (Luke 23:55, emphasis added). How could they possibly have seen this from a distance? Again, Lake tries to have his cake and eat it, using some of the biblical text but chopping out the bits that contradict his theory. This particular Lake holds no water!

Grave robbers?

Other ideas centre on the general theory that at some time between Friday evening and Sunday morning the body of Jesus was removed from the tomb. This would explain why it was empty when the women got there early on the Sunday morning: but *was* the grave robbed? Four suggestions have been made.

The first is that the body was stolen by 'a person or persons unknown', but nobody has come up with either motive or opportunity for this, let alone explained how they could have overcome an armed Roman guard. As for a motive, Jesus was not a wealthy man who might have valuable items buried with him; the evidence pointed in exactly the opposite direction. The Bible also tells us that the grave-clothes were left in the tomb, which means that all that was taken was a naked corpse. Why should anyone do this? As Sir J. N. D. Anderson, a former Professor of Oriental Law at the University of London, has said, *A Jew of that period could scarcely be suspected of stealing bodies on behalf of anatomical research!*

The second 'suspects' are *the Roman authorities*. They had an exclusive opportunity, as they were in charge of the tomb and its contents, but what motive could they have had? Nervous about the possibility of some strange goings-on, Pilate had insisted on maximum security, with an armed guard and his own seal (tampering with it would have meant execution). What could be gained by moving the body elsewhere? Pilate wanted to wash his hands of the case as soon as possible (and did so literally — see Matthew 27:24), so why would he want the body back? This idea collapses for another reason. If the Roman authorities had the body they would immediately have produced it when the disciples began preaching that Jesus was alive — and the Christian church would have collapsed on the spot.

The third suggestion is that the body was removed by *the Jewish religious authorities*. They would certainly have had a powerful motive. As Jesus had staked his integrity and identity on fulfilling his prophecy that he would be 'killed, and after three days rise again' (Mark 8:31), all they had to do was to keep the body under lock and key *for four days* and the whole 'Jesus movement' would be laughed out of court, with its leader exposed as a blasphemous fake.

Why did they not do this? When the disciples began preaching the resurrection of Jesus, the Jews had them arrested, imprisoned, flogged and executed, all of which would have been unnecessary if they had a body to produce. They could even have paraded it through the streets. As the Scottish theologian Professor Andrew Fairbairn has said, *The silence of the Jews is as significant as the speech of the Christians.*

The last suspects are *Jesus' own disciples*, but it is difficult to find either a motive or opportunity for them. Their leader's body had been buried in the tomb of a follower who was 'a respected member of the Council' (Mark 15:43). Why should they want to move it elsewhere? Opportunity is even more difficult to imagine. When Jesus was arrested his followers 'all left him and fled' (Mark 14:50) and when he was executed they hid behind locked doors 'for fear of the Jews' (John 20:19), terrified that they might be next on their hit list. Can we seriously imagine that this panic-stricken rabble suddenly plucked up the courage to go to the tomb, tackle an armed guard and risk the death penalty by breaking the governor's official seal on the rock, all for the purpose of taking possession of a dead body that was already in the safe keeping of a fellow Christian? If they did, why is there no record of them being charged with such serious offences?

The idea that the disciples stole the body faces at least two other problems. The first is *ethical*. These men had been powerfully influenced by Jesus and their lives had been transformed. As one of them was to write later, a person wanting to enjoy God's blessing on his life should 'keep his tongue from evil and his lips from speaking deceit' (1 Peter 3:10). It is inconceivable that men whose moral standards had been elevated to a level they had never known before should now base their entire teaching on a pack of lies they knew they had invented.

The second is *psychological*. Soon after the resurrection this handful of faithless and dejected men became a dynamic and fearless band of believers prepared to face persecution, imprisonment and execution rather than deny their convictions. When they were threatened with this kind of treatment and given strict instructions to stop preaching the resurrection of Jesus, they replied, *We must obey God rather than men* (Acts 5:29) and carried on preaching.

It was this transformation that convinced Charles Colson that the resurrection record was true. Colson was chief counsel to United States President Richard Nixon from 1969-1973 and was deeply involved in the Nixon administration's burglary of the Democrat Party's Watergate Office complex in Washington D.C. on 17 June 1972. The administration tried to cover up the crime, but in less than a month after criminal proceedings began three of those involved had gone to the Department of Justice to turn state evidence. Some time later, Colson wrote, *In my Watergate experience I saw the inability of men — powerful, highly motivated professionals — to hold together a conspiracy based on a lie ... Yet Christ's followers maintained to their grim deaths by execution that they had in fact seen Jesus Christ raised from the dead. There was no conspiracy ... Men do not give up comfort — and certainly not their lives — for what they know to be a lie.* This is hugely important. People may sometimes be willing to die for something they believe to be true (and countless fanatics have done so), *but nobody is prepared to die for something they know to be false.*

The witnesses

So much for alternative explanations of what may have happened — but they all cut across the Bible's strongest evidence that the resurrection of Jesus took place: the fact that he appeared to different people at different times in the days after his death and burial. Six independent witnesses record eleven separate appearances over a period of forty days. We have already touched on two of these, but they are included here so that we can see the whole picture.

- Mark tells us that after his resurrection Jesus *appeared first to Mary Magdalene, from whom he had cast out seven demons* (Mark 16:9).

- As a group of women were hurrying back to Jerusalem to tell the disciples about the empty tomb and what the angel had told them, *Jesus met them* (Matthew 28:9).

- Later that day, as two disciples were walking to Emmaus, a village about two miles from Jerusalem, *Jesus himself drew near and went with them* (Luke 24:15).

- After having an evening meal with Jesus, these two disciples rushed back to Jerusalem to tell the disciples, but before they could get their story out they were told, *The Lord has risen indeed, and has appeared to Simon!* (Luke 24:34).

- While they were excitedly discussing these extraordinary events, *Jesus himself stood among them, and said to them, "Peace to you!"* (Luke 24:36).

- A week later, when the disciples were hiding in the same house, *Jesus came and stood among them and said, "Peace be with you"* (John 20:26).

- Later, *Jesus revealed himself again to the disciples by the Sea of Tiberias* (John 21:1).

- There was one occasion when Jesus *appeared to more than five hundred brothers* (i.e. Christian believers) *at one time* (1 Corinthians 15:6).

- He also *appeared to James* (1 Corinthians 15:7).

- He appeared to eleven disciples when they were on a hillside in Galilee, and *when they saw him they worshipped him* (Matthew 28:17).

- Finally, Luke records that seven weeks after his resurrection Jesus *led them out as far as Bethany*, where, after giving them some final instructions, *he parted from them and was carried up into heaven* (Luke 24:50-51).

...and Paul

The earliest leaders of the Christian church became known as apostles, the primary qualification for which was to have been *a witness to his resurrection* (Acts 1:22). The apostle Paul was not included in any of these appearances; they all took place when he was on the brink of launching a murderous attack on the

Christian church. Yet years later, when he listed some of the people to whom Jesus appeared, he added, *Last of all ... he appeared also to me* (1 Corinthians 15:8). This was long after Jesus had ascended into heaven. As Paul immediately follows this by saying, *For I am the least of the apostles, unworthy to be called an apostle, because I persecuted the church of God* (1 Corinthians 15:9), he seems to be emphasizing God's grace to him in spite of his appalling record as a religious terrorist. What is certain is his claim that his experience of meeting with Jesus after his ascension was just as real and objective as those in the eleven other cases we have listed. When people in Corinth questioned his status and authority he had no hesitation in replying, *Am I not an apostle? Have I not seen Jesus our Lord?* (1 Corinthians 9:1).

Serial liars?

The evidence for Jesus being seen alive after his death *is* impressive, but this has not prevented it being questioned or denied. One approach bluntly claims that all the witnesses were lying. There is not a shred of evidence to support this idea —and what possible motive could they have had for doing so, when insisting they had seen him alive after death was certain to get them into serious trouble?

Paul's experience alone easily demolishes the idea that they were lying when they spoke of having met with Jesus after his resurrection. He was once a high-flying persecutor of the Christian church, *breathing threats and murder against the disciples of the Lord* (Acts

9:1), and licensed by the authorities to do so. After his conversion he could scarcely go anywhere without risking his life. In his own words, his work as an apostle brought him face to face with *danger from my own people, danger from Gentiles, danger in the city, danger in the wilderness, danger at sea, danger from false brothers* as well as having *many a sleepless night* and being *in hunger and thirst, often without food* and *in cold and exposure* (2 Corinthians 11:26-27). Would he have deliberately left himself open to all of this, and eventually be willing to die, for something he knew he had invented? Any competent psychologist would make pretty short work of that idea! People will sometimes lie to get out of trouble, but never to get into it.

Imagining things?

A second attack claims that the so-called sightings of Jesus were nothing more than hallucinations, brought on by the devastating trauma his followers experienced following his death. This is easy to claim but impossible to confirm. Hallucinations conform to certain laws, none of which applies in this case. As medical expert Professor A. Rendle Short puts it, *The resurrection appearances break every known law of visions.*

Firstly, hallucinations are usually associated with people who are *at least neurotic, if not actually psychotic*, but those who claimed to have seen Jesus included not only distressed women but the hot-tempered John, the aggressive Peter, an ordered civil servant like Matthew, a brilliant intellectual like Paul and a stubborn sceptic like Thomas. There is no hint in their stories that they were neurotic or psychotic.

Secondly, hallucinations usually take place in favourable circumstances and at times when the person concerned is wrapped in sentimental feelings or fond memories, yet hardly any of the reported appearances were in places where Jesus had spent time with his followers. He appeared in a garden, in a home, on a roadside, out in the country, on the seashore and on a hillside, and at many different times of day.

Thirdly, hallucinations are linked to a person's own subconscious ideas and are therefore intensely individual; but the Bible tells of Jesus meeting not only with individuals but with two, three, seven and even over 500 at the same time. Many people can truthfully tell of having seen something unusual and even unique, but for over 500 people to have an identical hallucination at the same time is unheard of. A friend of mine speaking at a school assembly of 200 students suddenly produced a pair of scissors and cut the head teacher's tie in pieces (by prior arrangement!). My friend then turned to the assembly and said something like this: *Imagine that on the way home you meet a friend who is not here this morning and you tell her that you saw the speaker at assembly chop up the head teacher's tie. She would think you were pulling her leg. But suppose that three other classmates met her and told her the same thing, and that on the following day all thirty students in your class told her they saw it happen. Now imagine that all 200 of you in this hall told her the same story. Surely she would then have no reason for doubting? Over 500 people saying they had seen Jesus alive after death is powerful evidence that they were telling the truth.*

Referring to these 500 people Paul added, *most of whom are still alive* (1 Corinthians 15:6). People did not have to take Paul's word for it. Over half of this large crowd could be interrogated and every person would have told the same story. The problem for the sceptic is not to explain why so many people had this hallucination, but why there was not a single person in that large crowd who did not have it! The American theologian J. Gresham Machen, a firm believer in the resurrection, once wryly suggested that if all the people who claimed they had seen Jesus alive after his death were hallucinating it would mean that *if there had been a good neurologist for Peter and others to consult there would never have been a Christian church*.

Wishful thinking?

A third attack suggests that these witnesses so badly wanted Jesus back that they were overwhelmed by wishful thinking and treated their imagination as if it were reality. Countless people still talk of seeing Elvis Presley alive though he died in 1977. The Elvis Sighting Bulletin Board has a web site which claims to keep visitors aware of his movements so that they will not be alarmed by seeing 'The King' at their local supermarket or swimming in a neighbour's pool.

The resurrection of Jesus is a different matter altogether, not least because *his followers did not expect him to come alive again*. When the first women went to the tomb it was to embalm him, not to embrace him. When Mary told the disciples they had seen Jesus *they would not believe it* (Mark 16:11). One of them (Thomas) went further: *Unless I see in his hands the mark of the nails, and place my finger into the mark of the nails, and place my hand into his side, I will never believe* (John 20:25); not much wishful thinking there! Mark even tells us that on another occasion Jesus appeared to them as they were having a meal and *he rebuked them for their unbelief and hardness of heart, because they had not believed those who saw him after he had risen* (Mark 16:14). Several weeks later, even when most of his followers had become completely convinced, *some doubted* (Matthew 28:17). None of these incidents sound like people jumping to emotionally triggered conclusions! Paul reports seeing Jesus a long time after the initial emotion surrounding the resurrection had died down and at a time when he was convinced that the whole thing was a pack of lies. Not only was the resurrection of Jesus the last thing he expected, *it was the last thing he wanted*, so he can hardly be charged with wishful thinking that eventually led to hallucination. Those first Christians were utterly sceptical until they faced a fact that could not be denied.

Ghost story?

The nineteenth-century theologian Karl Theodor Keim tried another attack by suggesting that the people who claimed Jesus had come back to life had seen a spirit or ghost, but when set along what the Bible says this idea also collapses in a heap. When he appeared to the two disciples who were walking to Emmaus, he shared a meal with them, *took the bread and blessed and broke it and gave it to them* (Luke 24:30). This one incident 'puts the kibosh' on Keim, as ghosts are not in the habit of passing food around!

When Jesus met the disciples in their hideout, they were terrified, but he told them, *Why are you troubled, and why do doubts arise in your hearts? See my hands and my feet, that it is I myself. Touch me, and see. For a spirit does not have flesh and bones as you see that I have* (Luke 24:38-39). When they still *did not believe it because of joy and amazement* he asked if they had any food in the house, and when they gave him a piece of broiled fish *he took it and ate it in their presence* (Luke 24:41-43, NIV). By appealing to their senses — sight, hearing and touch — Jesus wanted to show them that he was not a disembodied spirit.

He took the same approach with the doubting Thomas: *Put your finger here, and see my hands; and put out your hand, and place it in my side. Do not disbelieve, but believe* (John 20:27). Later, on the seashore at Galilee, Jesus invited seven of his followers to *Come and have breakfast* (John 21:12). This so impressed Peter that he later referred to the apostles as those *who ate and drank with him after he rose from the dead* (Acts 10:41).

This all tells us that when Jesus rose from the dead he had a *physical* body, yet one without the usual limitations. His transformed body moved away from the grave-clothes without disturbing them. He could walk through walls, yet eat food. He could appear and disappear at will. He was able to enter a room without passing through a door or a window, yet the crucifixion scars on his hands, feet and side were visible. This could explain why there were times when those who met him did not always recognize him immediately, yet always did so eventually. His resurrection body was identifiable with his pre-death body, yet not identical to it. The fact that we cannot explain this is no reason for denying it. The resurrection of Jesus is clearly not a ghost story.

Author John Benton is right when he says, *For 2,000 years people have been trying to come up with alternative explanations for the resurrection accounts and nothing even approaching a viable alternative has ever been produced. That is something which speaks for itself.*

Reinforcing the record

There are four easily missed facts that give the resurrection story a further ring of truth. The first is that there is no description of the actual event. This might seem to be a weak link, but is exactly the opposite. Had the apostles invented the resurrection, it is difficult to imagine them missing the opportunity of including an eyewitness account of it and decorating it with extravagant descriptions. Instead, they say nothing about it. Their silence is significant.

Secondly, when Peter went into the tomb on the Sunday morning, *He saw the linen cloths lying there, and the face cloth, which had been on Jesus' head, not lying with the linen cloths but folded up in a place by itself* (John 20:6-7). Moments later, John confirmed Peter's findings. At first glance, describing how the grave-clothes were lying seems irrelevant, but this is not so. The word 'lying' (used twice of the linen cloths) translates a word commonly used of something done in a very orderly way, while the phrase about the face cloth being 'folded up' means something like 'twirled about itself'. The grave-clothes looked like the empty chrysalis of a caterpillar's cocoon. This would not have been the case if the swoon theory is true and Jesus had recovered from a near-death experience and wrestled out of grave-clothes smothered in substances which would have stuck to the body, as one writer says, 'not less firmly than lead'. Nor can we imagine him stopping to tidy them up as if he were leaving his bedroom for a day's work. Would grave robbers (Romans, Jews or disciples) increase the risk of being caught by taking time to tidy everything up before they rushed out?

Instead, the grave-clothes looked exactly as they would have done had they subsided when the body moved away. This was the immediate effect they had on John, who *saw and believed* (John 20:8). He became the first person to believe that Jesus had risen from the dead, and what convinced him was not merely the absence of the body but the way the grave-clothes were left.

Thirdly, the resurrection story gains credibility from the fact that the first time Jesus appeared it was to a woman. This may seem irrelevant to those of us living in the modern Western world, but in the Middle East 2,000 years ago it was hugely significant as women counted for very little. As Michael Green says, *They were nobodies; they were goods and chattels; they could in some circumstances be offered for sale;* **they could not bear witness in a court of law** (emphasis added). This may partly explain why, when Mary and the other women told the disciples they had seen Jesus, their story *seemed to them an idle tale, and they did not believe them* (Luke 24:11). They reacted like the second-century philosopher Celsus, who ridiculed the resurrection as something based on the word of a 'hysterical female'. The last thing the disciples expected was that Jesus would rise from the dead and they were not going to take a woman's word for it. If they had invented the resurrection story there is no way they would have given females such a leading role.

Fourthly, although all four Gospels give an account of the resurrection it is impossible to arrange their accounts into exact chronological order. What seems like another weakness turns out to be exactly the opposite. If the four writers had invented the story they would have made sure that their versions fitted together perfectly so that they all stayed 'on message'.

Instead, they are very different from each other, though unanimous that the grave was empty and that Jesus had been seen alive.

Witnesses in a court of law may all give truthful accounts of an incident as they saw it, yet their testimonies may emphasize different details without contradicting the essential truth of what happened. On the other hand, criminals may get together to concoct a story that would hold together when giving evidence in court. Newspaper reports of a sporting event can differ so much that I sometimes wonder when reading them whether the reporters saw the same game — but they all report the final score accurately. In the same way, the four major resurrection accounts differ in the details but not in the final fact: Jesus rose from the dead.

The terrorist

One of the most significant statements on the resurrection of Jesus that has ever been recorded comes from the pen of the apostle Paul — and his background made him a very unlikely candidate. Given the name Saul at birth, he began life around A.D. 10, in Tarsus, a university town and commercial centre in Mersin Province, Turkey, but at that time the capital city of the Roman province of Cilicia in Asia Minor. His parents were of solid Jewish stock and could trace their ancestry back to the elite Old Testament tribe of Benjamin. He was steeped in

Judaism from birth and when eight days old was circumcised according to ancient Jewish law.

After a thoroughly religious education in Tarsus he moved to Jerusalem, where he studied under Gamaliel, one of the greatest ever Jewish scholars. While still a student, Saul joined the strictest sect in the Jewish religion and became a dedicated Pharisee. As such, he accepted the entire Old Testament as God's law and strongly opposed all who took a looser, liberal approach to the ancient text.

When the Christian church came into existence he saw it as a direct threat to his Jewish faith. He believed that one day God would send his promised Messiah (God's anointed representative) to fulfil all the Old Testament promises God made to his people and ultimately to set up a perfect and everlasting kingdom. About 400 years after the final Old Testament prophecy, Jesus suddenly burst on the scene, claiming that he was the promised Messiah and that all these prophecies referred to him (see Luke 4:16-30). Those first Christians believed not only that he was telling the truth but also that after his death he had come back to life, clinching his claim that he was both man and God.

This was the tipping point. The idea that a carpenter's son from a small town (Nazareth) not even mentioned in the Old Testament — and who had been executed as a common criminal — was both human and divine was more than Saul could stand. Determined to wipe out those who were now worshipping someone he rated as a blasphemous imposter, he embarked on a search and destroy mission against Christians wherever they could be found.

Beginning at Jerusalem, he flushed believers out of their homes and had them thrown into prison (see Acts 8:3). Later, armed with arrest warrants from the high priest, he travelled to foreign cities as far away as Damascus, in Syria. Wherever he found Christians he dragged them before local courts, tried to force them to blaspheme, or in his 'raging fury' (Acts 26:11) hauled them back to Jerusalem for punishment, which at times meant the death sentence. The first was carried out on Stephen, an early Christian preacher — 'and Saul approved of his execution' (Acts 8:1).

Then something amazing happened — *Saul became a Christian!* He became utterly convinced that in attacking the Christian faith he had been fighting not *for* the truth but *against* it: Jesus *was* God; he *did* come into the world to bring men and women back into a living relationship with their Creator; his death *was* an act of amazing love on his part, atoning for other people's sins; *and he did rise again from the dead*, becoming a living Saviour to all who put their trust in him.

What is more, the persecutor became a preacher of the faith he once tried to destroy. Under his adopted name of Paul he wrote more about the resurrection than any other New Testament writer and in one passage makes its importance crystal clear. It will be useful to spell it out in full before unpacking its meaning:

> Now if Christ is proclaimed as raised from the dead, how can some of you say that there is no resurrection of the dead? But if there is no resurrection of the dead, then not even Christ has been raised. And if Christ has not been raised, then our preaching is in vain and your faith is in vain. We are even found to be misrepresenting God, because we testified about God that he raised Christ, whom he did not raise if it is true that the dead are not raised. For if the dead are not raised, not even Christ has been raised. And if Christ has not been raised, your faith is futile and you are still in your sins. Then those also who have fallen asleep in Christ have perished. If in this life only we have hoped in Christ, we are of all people most to be pitied (1 Corinthians 15:12-19).

Life after death?

Philosopher Bertrand Russell had a straightforward view on life after death: *there is no such thing.* In his own words, *When I die I shall rot, and nothing of my ego shall survive.* This is known as annihilationism, which teaches that life on earth is all we can expect as there is nothing beyond the grave; our spirits will be snuffed out like a candle the moment we die and our bodies will gradually disintegrate.

Paul makes it clear that if this were true Christianity would collapse, as it is based on the *bodily* resurrection of Jesus: *Now if Christ is proclaimed as raised from the dead, how can some of you say that there is no resurrection of the dead? But if there is no resurrection of the dead, then not even Christ has been raised* (vv. 12-13). Paul is just clearing the way for what follows by making the point we established earlier: if Jesus is still in the grave the Christian faith is nothing more than a man-made ethical or religious system — and built on a monumental lie.

Hot air?

Paul goes on to list some of the things that follow if Jesus never came back to life, and the first is this: *then our preaching is in vain* (v. 14). Paul is writing as one of the apostles, men who had seen Jesus after his resurrection and had been commissioned to take his message to the world. When Paul says that without the resurrection their preaching would have been 'in vain' he is not saying that it would have lacked style or 'pizzazz', but that it would have been utterly useless. The word 'vain' translates the Greek *kenos,* which means 'empty or hollow'. If Jesus had not come back to life any preaching notes the apostles might have used would not have been worth the papyrus on which they were written.

Paul is not exaggerating. When the apostle Peter preached the Christian church's first recorded sermon (see Acts 2:1-41), over half of it was taken up with the resurrection of Jesus, the key phrase being *God raised him up* (Acts 2:24, 32). From then on, all of the apostles' preaching was centred on the resurrection: *And with great power the apostles were giving their testimony to the resurrection of the Lord Jesus* (Acts 4:33). Just before the passage we are examining, Paul emphasized as being 'of first importance' the three-part fact that Jesus died, was buried, and *was raised on the third day* (1 Corinthians 15:3-4). By saying that these events were 'of first importance', Paul was telling his readers that whatever else he taught them, whether about corporate worship, personal morality, business ethics, family life or anything else, *nothing* matched the importance of the death, burial and resurrection of Jesus Christ.

We dare not miss this! The first Christian preachers fell foul of the religious establishment not because they were promoting a new style of worship or suggesting a different approach to moral issues, but *because they were teaching the people and proclaiming in Jesus the resurrection from the dead* (Acts 4:2). This was not a sensational 'extra' to attract a crowd; it was the heart and soul of the entire message of not only the apostles, but also of every New Testament writer. The centre of gravity in their teaching was not an ethic but an event and if the event never took place we can feed the New Testament to the shredder. As the Scottish scholar James S. Stewart wrote of the resurrection of Jesus, *This is no appendix to the faith. This **is** the faith.*

All in the same boat

Paul presses on: *and your faith is in vain* (v. 14). The issue was not confined to the first Christian preachers, but to everybody (and very soon there were thousands) who heard them preach and then declared themselves Christians. If Jesus never rose from the dead, not only were the apostles preaching empty nonsense, but all who believed their message had been hoodwinked and were pinning their hopes to a mirage. A little earlier, Paul tells the Christians at Corinth that the gospel (climaxing in the resurrection) was something *on which you have taken your stand* (v. 1, NIV). The Christian faith claims to be built on facts, but if the greatest 'fact' was fiction those early believers were not 'standing' anywhere; their feet were dangling in mid-air, with nothing to support them.

The same thing would be equally true of every Christian believer from then onwards, including the millions alive today, who form the largest religious grouping the world has ever known — and there are other dramatic implications. Without the resurrection of Jesus, the millions of Christian martyrs (more in the twentieth century than in any previous one) died for a cause that had no foundation; and the great Reformers, people like John Calvin, Thomas Cranmer, John Knox, Martin Luther and William Tyndale, would have been better employed wrecking the church rather than reforming it, as it had been built on a pack of lies. It would also mean that every Christian church building, from the most magnificent cathedral to the smallest mission hall, is a monument to a myth; that every minister who teaches the Bible as the Word of God is peddling perversion; that every Christian service is a farce; and that every Easter Day commemorates an event that never happened. Claiming that Jesus is now nothing more than a handful of bones and dust buried somewhere in the Middle East carries some pretty hefty baggage.

Caught in the act?

Paul's next statement is even more serious: *We are even found to be misrepresenting God, because we testified about God that he raised Christ, whom he did not raise if it is true that the dead are not raised* (v. 15). The word 'found' means being found out, like a criminal caught red-handed, while 'testified' is the word that would be used about giving evidence in a court of law. When we take on board the fact that 'testified about God' literally means 'testified *against* God' we begin to see the profound implications of the statement Paul is making here. We could paraphrase it like this: 'We are preaching that God raised Jesus from the dead, but if the dead are not raised we are swearing on oath that God did something, whereas we know that he did no such thing.' To swear on oath that a person did something we know perfectly well they did not is perjury, a serious offence carrying a heavy penalty, but it is as nothing compared to knowingly lying about God.

For Paul to have done such a thing would at the very least have been breathtakingly arrogant. As *a Hebrew of Hebrews* (Philippians 3:5), belief in God ran in his veins and as a brilliant Old Testament scholar his knowledge about him would have been exceptional. He believed that God was the Creator and Ruler of the universe (see Genesis 1:1 and 1 Chronicles 21:11), that he was utterly holy (see Isaiah 6:1, 3), that he was all-knowing (see Job 37:16) and that he was the Judge of all the earth (see Psalm 7:11). What is more, Paul taught elsewhere that the day was coming when *each of us will give an account of himself to God* (Romans 14:12). It is simply impossible to imagine Paul deliberately testifying against God, let alone basing his entire ministry on a blasphemous lie.

Column 9

After underlining a point he had made earlier — *For if the dead are not raised, not even Christ has been raised* (v. 16) — Paul takes things even further: *And if Christ has not been raised, your faith is futile and you are still in your sins* (v. 17). The word 'futile' is subtly different from the word 'vain' which he had used earlier about the apostles' preaching and their hearers' faith; it translates *mataia*, which refers to something that is useless because it fails to do what it promises. Discovering why Paul uses it here takes us to the very heart of the Christian message, which explains why Jesus died in the first place.

From 1948-1954 I worked in the Registrar-General's Office on my native island of Guernsey and I will never forget my early reaction when reading death certificates. The first eight columns (date of death, name, age, details of parents and so on) were straightforward, but I often became riveted by the next one — 'Certified cause of death'. The day before the first date on the certificate the person concerned had been alive — and may have seemed in no immediate danger of dying — but Column 9 told me what had changed everything. Over fifty years later I can still remember some of the words it used. Some were ominously complicated — 'Arteriosclerotic degeneration of the myocardium' or 'Pulmonary embolism and bronchopneumonia' — but in other cases there was just one woeful word: 'Cancer'. Whatever the words in Column 9, they defined what turned living beings into corpses. *But why?* Why does death come to everybody, whatever their status or station in life, from kings to commoners and the nobility to 'nonentities'? Why is the whole world like a hospital, with every person in it a terminal patient? The answer is the key to Paul's teaching about the resurrection of Jesus.

The Bible says that Adam, the first human being, was created *in the image of God* (Genesis 1:27). This does not mean that he was created in God's size or shape as *God is spirit* (John 4:24) and has neither, but that he was created as a moral and spiritual being, a perfect though human reflection of God's holy character. Yet he was not like a mechanical toy which God had wound up and which could do only what had been programmed in. He and his God-given partner Eve were perfectly free to obey or disobey their Creator, and for some time they chose to live in perfect obedience to God's will, enjoying in full all that he had lovingly and generously provided.

Then disaster struck. In the Bible's words, *sin came into the world ... and death through sin* (Romans 5:12). When Adam and Eve disobeyed God the result was catastrophic and is summed up in one word: 'death'. It is vital at this point to realize that *in the Bible death never means termination. It always means separation.* The death penalty their sin incurred was 'double-barrelled'; it meant both spiritual death (their souls were immediately separated from God, ending the perfect relationship they had previously enjoyed with him) and physical death (their souls would eventually be separated from their bodies).

Their sin changed the whole course of human history, because as the representative head of the human race Adam's guilt and corruption were passed on to his successors. Adam's children were born *in his own likeness, after his image* (Genesis 5:3), that is to say, in the same fallen, corrupt spiritual state as their father — and with the same deadly result for them and for all his descendants. As Paul himself puts it, 'In Adam *all* die' (1 Corinthians 15:22). The fact that I am dying as I write these words and that you are dying as you read them shows that the human race is a united whole; Adam is the root and we are the branches. Nor is there any point in protesting that we should not be punished for Adam's disobedience, as we have enough of our own to condemn us: *If we say we have no sin, we deceive ourselves, and the truth is not in us* (1 John 1:8). The Bible also teaches that sin cuts a person off from God both in this life and in the one to come. The Bible's most common word for this eternal disaster is 'hell' and Jesus spoke more about this than he did about heaven, constantly warning people of its terrible reality.

The substitute

Unless we grasp the truth about sin and its effects we can never begin to understand the meaning of the birth, life, death and resurrection of Jesus, who *came into the world to save sinners* (1 Timothy 1:15). His birth was normal, but his conception was not. He was conceived in the womb of his virgin mother by a miraculous act of God, something beyond the laws of nature. This meant that Jesus was both human and divine, as fully man as if he were not God and as fully God as if he were not man. The Bible then shows that his life was unique in human culture, not merely the finest, but flawless: *holy, innocent, unstained* (Hebrews 7:26). This means that he was not subject to what the Bible calls *the law of sin and death* (Romans 8:2), which condemns the rest of the human race. Yet in order to save sinners he deliberately laid down his life, and in dying on the cross bore in his own body and spirit the double death penalty others deserved. As the Bible puts it, he died *the righteous for the unrighteous, that he might bring us to God* (1 Peter 3:18). He paid in full the penalty others had incurred, removing the barrier that separated them from God so enabling God to forgive them and welcome them into his family for ever. His resurrection proved that that penalty had been paid and that all who put their trust in Jesus receive *the free gift of God ... eternal life* (Romans 6:23).

This is the very heart of the Bible's teaching and of the apostles' message — and the resurrection sealed its truth. Yet as Paul made clear to his readers, if Jesus had not been raised, *you are still in your sins*. However sincere their faith, they remained unforgiven for ever and condemned to 'eternal punishment' (Matthew 25:46) in the life to come. If Jesus had not been raised, claiming that their sins were forgiven and that they had come into an eternal relationship with God would show that they were living in cloud cuckoo land.

The destiny of the dead

Paul now adds another obvious fact: if Jesus did not rise from the dead, *those also who have fallen asleep in Christ have perished* (v. 18). To 'fall asleep in Christ' was a phrase the early church used about Christians dying. As a person who is asleep still exists, so does a person who has died, and those early Christians believed that to die 'in Christ' was to die united to him in his resurrection and so, beyond death, to share eternal life with him in heaven. Yet if Jesus Christ had not been raised to life, his death would have accomplished nothing and those who had put their trust in him would be 'lost', with nobody to stand between them and a holy God on the day of judgement. They would have gone through life hoping for everlasting glory in heaven, yet died doomed to everlasting misery in hell.

In 1813 the young American missionary Adoniram Judson went to work in Burma (now Myanmar) as a missionary. There he faced fierce opposition, was plagued by tropical diseases and suffered the premature deaths of his first and second wives and three young children. During the first Anglo-Burmese war he was tortured and held for well over a year in a vermin-ridden 'death prison'. Sometimes he was suspended by his fettered feet, with only his head and shoulders touching the ground. It took him twenty-four years to translate the Bible into Burmese and he also compiled the first Burmese-English dictionary. His work-rate was phenomenal and when he died at the age of sixty-one he left behind 100 churches and over 8,000 believers. Shortly before his death, he said, *I am not tired of my work, neither am I tired of the world; yet, when Christ calls me home, I shall go with gladness.* Yet if Jesus did not rise from the dead and ascend to heaven to receive Christian believers, Judson's labours were pointless and his hope of spending eternity with Christ was utterly futile.

Wasted world view

Paul then adds another implication: *If in this life only we have hoped in Christ, we are of all people most to be pitied* (v. 19). Paul's point is clear. If this world is all there is, it is pointless for Christians to live in the context of one to come. We might as well live it up to the full while we can, squeezing every drop of pleasure we can out of the few years we spend on earth, regardless of any moral or eternal considerations. If we die as animals, why not live as animals? Corliss Lamont, a contemporary humanist, cheerfully recited, *While we're here, let's live in clover; for when we're dead, we're dead all over.* Paul recognized that many took this approach and he quoted an ancient saying with which millions today happily agree: *Let us eat and drink, for tomorrow we die* (1 Corinthians 15:32).

Yet Paul and his fellow Christians took a completely different line. Their philosophy and lifestyles were geared to the conviction that this life is a preparation for one to come. In an uncertain world they had their eyes fixed on heaven, *the city that has foundations, whose designer and builder is God* (Hebrews 11:10). They were convinced that *the world is passing away along with its desires, but whoever does the will of God abides for ever* (1 John 2:17).

Above all, they were certain that when Jesus told his followers just before his death, *I go to prepare a place for you* (John 14:2), he was telling the truth and referring to the glories of heaven, where *death shall be no more, neither shall there be mourning nor crying nor*

47

pain any more (Revelation 21:4). But if Jesus did not rise from the dead he was not going anywhere to prepare anything for anybody. Instead he would simply rot away in his grave, just like everyone else.

Paul had other reasons for saying that if this were true, Christians were to be 'pitied'. In those early years, Christians often suffered fierce opposition and persecution because of their faith. According to *Foxe's Book of Martyrs* John was the only apostle who died of natural causes, all the others being executed because of their commitment to Jesus Christ. The apostle Peter is said to have been crucified upside down following the execution of his wife. Successive Roman emperors had Christians sewn up in the skins of wild animals and thrown to dogs. Others were tortured, beheaded, crucified or boiled alive. In the first three hundred years of the Christian church, at least 10,000 believers were put to death for no other reason than their faith in Jesus Christ. Paul himself was *in danger every hour* (1 Corinthians 15:30) and says he had suffered *imprisonments, with countless beatings*, was 'beaten with rods' and 'stoned', and had gone through *toil and hardship, through many a sleepless night, in hunger and thirst, often without food, in cold and exposure* (2 Corinthians 11:23-27). He was eventually taken to Rome, where tradition says he was beheaded on the directions of the Emperor Nero. Why would he deliberately expose himself to all of this if he knew that Jesus was dead?

Two thousand years later, countless Christians are still being pressurized, persecuted and put to death because of their faith. There are countries in which to convert to Christianity from another religion is effectively to sign one's death warrant. A recent report from the World Evangelical Alliance Religious Commission concludes: *Literally hundreds of thousands of people today are being killed, brutalized, sold as slaves, imprisoned, tortured, threatened, discriminated against and arrested solely because they are Christians. They are being subjected to persecution and suffering, the extent of which we can hardly begin to comprehend, because of their faith ... Incredibly, more than 200 million people in over 60 nations are being denied their basic human rights for one reason only: they are Christians.*

Yet if Jesus was not raised from the dead all this pain and suffering is pointless, and all these sufferers are victims of a gigantic hoax. No wonder Paul says that if the resurrection never took place Christians are 'of all people most to be pitied'.

New men, new movement

Professor F. F. Bruce claimed, *If Jesus had not risen from the dead, we should probably have never heard of him.* He may be right. What is certain is that around A.D. 32 a dynamic new movement sprang into existence, beginning with a handful of men who believed Jesus had risen from the dead. A few days earlier they had been terrified at what might happen to them as followers of Jesus, yet after the resurrection they came out of hiding and risked their lives by preaching that Jesus was alive. Their chief spokesman was Peter, who seven weeks earlier had not only deserted Jesus but even denied that he knew him (see Luke 22:54-62). Yet when he and John were arrested and interrogated, their accusers were amazed at 'the boldness of Peter and John' (Acts 4:13). All the apostles experienced the same change and not even the threat of imprisonment or execution could stop them. They had been demoralized and distraught, now they were confident and courageous, and their amazing transformation from cowardice to courage persuaded Professor J. N. D. Anderson that it was *by far and away the strongest circumstantial evidence for the resurrection.*

They were soon joined by countless others. On their very first day of public preaching about three thousand (Acts 2:41) were added to their number. Soon, *the number of the men came to about five thousand* (Acts 4:4). The church's rapid growth continued in spite of constant persecution, first locally, then throughout the Roman Empire. The Emperor Nero made Christians the scapegoats for a disastrous fire that swept through Rome in A.D. 64 and he had them savagely tortured, burnt alive or fed to lions. Countless others were executed for their faith over the next three centuries, yet their courage and conviction led to so many new believers replacing them that the third-century theologian Tertullian, himself a convert from paganism, famously said, *The blood of the martyrs is the seed of the church.*

By the early part of the fourth century, Christianity had spread so far and penetrated society so deeply that in A.D. 313 Emperor Constantine, who had also professed faith, declared Christianity a recognized religion of the Roman Empire, and by A.D. 395 it had become the only official state religion. There is a good case for saying that this weakened the Christian cause rather than strengthened it, by making Christian faith cultural rather than personal, but it is still amazing that within four hundred years it had gained such recognition by the state that had killed its founder.

What was the key to this movement's staggering growth? It taught nothing new about the nature of God, the origin of man or the creation of the universe, nor was it revolutionary on social issues. Just one thing triggered it off: *the resurrection of Jesus*. Historian Robert Linder puts it perfectly: *It is hard to conceive that there would have been any Christianity without a firm belief by the early disciples in the bodily resurrection of Jesus. They were convinced that their master had conquered death and had appeared to many of them in person. Only this resurrection faith explains how the small, motley, demoralized group which Jesus left on earth after his reported ascension could have developed the enthusiasm to sweep all obstacles before them in their bold world-wide mission. A few disheartened followers were transformed into the most dynamic movement in the history of mankind.*

Changes

This new faith sparked off dramatic changes in religious customs. In obedience to the fourth of the Ten Commandments (Exodus 20:8-11) Jews observed the Sabbath (Saturday) as a day of rest and worship, yet the first Christians, who were almost all devout Jews, abandoned the Sabbath and met together on Sunday, 'the first day of the week' (Acts 20:7). They did this to commemorate the day on which Jesus rose from the dead. There is no parallel in history but a simple illustration reflects something of the same principle. On 9 May 1945 my native island of Guernsey was liberated from German occupation and my father was among huge crowds who saw those first British troops land. When I returned to Guernsey three months later (I had been a war-time evacuee) I could never have convinced my father and the thousands who saw it happen that the liberation of the island had never taken place, nor in the years that followed could I have persuaded them that the annual Liberation Day service held in St Peter Port's Town Church celebrated a non-event.

There were other significant changes. For almost two thousand years, circumcision had been the sign of entry into the family of God. The first Christians immediately replaced it with baptism and Paul explains why: *We were buried therefore with him* (Jesus) *by baptism into death, in order that, just as Christ was raised from the dead by the glory of the Father, we too might walk in newness of life* (Romans 6:4). Overturning twenty centuries of tradition was a massive move — and it was the resurrection of Jesus that brought it about.

Again, for centuries Jews had kept the Passover feast to commemorate the liberation of their forefathers after 400 years of slavery in Egypt, but those early Christians replaced it with what is now called Holy Communion, the Lord's Supper or the Breaking of Bread. This was instituted by Jesus at a final meal with his disciples when he explained that the bread and wine symbolized his body and blood, then said from then on they were to, *Do this in remembrance of me* (Luke 22:19). Soon, we find the early Christians doing so regularly, *with glad and sincere hearts* (Acts 2:46, NIV).

The Christian Sunday, baptism and Holy Communion are all linked to the resurrection of Jesus and none of them makes any sense without it. As someone has rightly said, *The Christian church has resurrection written all over it.*

The ongoing legacy

Today, there are over two billion professing Christians in the world and the number is growing by thousands every day. This represents impressive growth, which in China, Korea and South America is redrawing the world's religious map. Yet the progress of Christianity has not always been steady. There have been great forward surges, such as the sixteenth-century Reformation and other times of 'awakening' and revival, but also periods of serious decline and shameful episodes such as the notorious Crusades from the eleventh to thirteenth centuries. Yet the Christian movement continues to grow and despite its wobbles and weaknesses it has been an immense influence for good throughout the world.

When we think in historical terms about the foundation of schools, hospitals and institutions to care for the homeless and destitute, the abolition of the slave trade or improving the conditions of those working in mills and mines or suffering appalling conditions in prisons, no organization did more. Today, Christians around the world are shining examples in caring for the blind and the deaf, the orphaned and the widowed, the poor and the hungry, the deprived and disadvantaged, the homeless and the helpless, the sick and the dying.

Many people of other religious faiths, and some with no declared faith at all, are involved in similar commendable work; but no other group contributes more to human well-being — and none has a better reason for doing so. Why sacrifice anything to meet the needs of others if in the long run humankind is doomed to extinction and nothing we do will make any eternal difference? The impetus driving generations of Christians in the service of others has been the assurance of the resurrection of Jesus, which has given them a dynamic love for others that has no equal. If the resurrection never took place it is difficult to explain all of this, or even how the Christian church got started at all. As the American preacher D. James Kennedy put it: *The Grand Canyon wasn't caused by an Indian dragging a stick, and the Christian church wasn't created by a myth.*

The evidence for the resurrection of Jesus has convinced many eminent men well qualified to assess the truth. In a document found among his private papers, Lord Lyndhurst, one of the greatest minds in English legal history, wrote, *I know pretty well what evidence is; and I tell you, such evidence as that for the resurrection has never broken down yet.* Lord Darling, a former Chief Justice of England, concludes: *There exists such overwhelming evidence, positive and negative, factual and circumstantial, that no intelligent jury could fail to bring in a verdict that the resurrection is true.*

The God-man

Before we go any further it is important to remember that in every respect Jesus was a genuine human being. He was *descended from David according to the flesh* (Romans 1:3) and though he had no human father he was *born of woman* (Galatians 4:4). As an infant, he needed to be nursed, fed, washed and trained like any other child. He passed through his teenage years into manhood and for about thirty years was virtually unknown. You would probably not have picked him out in a crowd. He had emotional ups and downs; we are told that he 'rejoiced' (Luke 10:21) and that he was *greatly distressed and troubled* (Mark 14:33). He knew what it was to be *tempted as we are* — though uniquely *without sin* (Hebrews 4:15). Just as his conception was unique, so was the quality of his life. His voluntary death in the place of others, bearing the penalty for their sin, was also unparalleled.

However, the resurrection takes us beyond his humanity. The Bible says that in his resurrection he was *declared to be the Son of God in power* (Romans 1:4). This does not mean that the resurrection *made* Jesus the Son of God: *it demonstrated that he was.* The resurrection is publicly announced proof of something that has been true for all eternity, not of something that happened on the first Easter Day. The resurrection declared the true identity of Jesus. The Bible tells us that he was both 'Son of Man' (John 1:51) and 'Son of God'. 'Son of Man' declares his humanity; 'Son of God' declares his divinity. 'Son of God' is another way of saying that Jesus is one of three persons in the Godhead (the Father, the Son and the Holy Spirit). However mysterious this may seem to our finite way of thinking, *the Bible is crystal clear in declaring that Jesus is God.*

So what?

This has momentous implications and the person who asks, 'So what?' is not thinking straight. There are at least three obvious things that follow from the fact that Jesus is God.

Firstly, *all his claims are true.* He said, *I am the light of the world. Whoever follows me will not walk in darkness, but will have the light of life* (John 8:12). This destroys the popular idea that everyone has the right to choose their own moral standards and that no one else has the right to contradict them. Instead, Jesus said that in his earthly life he reflected the nature of God, in whom *is no darkness at all* (1 John 1:5).

On another occasion he claimed, *I am the way, and the truth, and the life. No one comes to the Father except through me* (John 14:6). Nobody else has ever made a credible claim like this, yet Jesus had no hesitation in saying that he was the only means of entering into a right relationship with God. This flatly contradicts the popular idea that 'all religions lead to God'. The way to get right with God is not by following a philosophical system, nor by going through religious rituals or ceremonies, nor by 'doing the best we can'. The only way is by personal commitment to Jesus Christ, who *came into the world to save sinners* (1 Timothy 1:15) and laid down his own perfect life in their place and on their behalf, *the righteous for the unrighteous, that he might bring us to God* (1 Peter 3:18).

Secondly, *all his warnings are true.* God the Father sent Jesus into the world on a rescue mission, *not ... to condemn the world, but in order that the world might be saved through him* (John 3:17). Left to ourselves we are in appalling danger, as Jesus made clear time and again. He taught that *everyone who commits sin is a slave to sin* (John 8:34). People often treat sin lightly, but Jesus said it is not a toy but a tyrant that imprisons us and from which we have no power to escape. The person who refuses to believe this is simply in denial.

Jesus gave a similar warning when he said that he had come into the world *to seek and to save the lost* (Luke 19:10). This not only underlines our present condition but tells us that if nothing is done about it we will be lost for ever, paying the horrific penalty that a holy God rightly demands for sin.

Jesus made this even clearer when he declared that when the entire human race stands before him on the Day of Judgement he will say to those who did not trust him, *Depart from me, you cursed, into the eternal fire prepared for the devil and his angels* (Matthew 25:41).

Another warning is linked to a person's understanding of who Jesus is. Having identified himself in the way we have seen, he told his hearers, *Unless you believe that I am he you will die in your sins* (John 8:24). To die 'in your sins' means to die with every one of your sins (of thought, word and deed) counting against you when you stand before a God who says of heaven that *nothing unclean will ever enter it* (Revelation 21:27). What is more, Jesus told those who were rejecting him, *You will die in your sin* (John 8:21). Men and women will be condemned not only because of an accumulation of sinful thoughts, words and deeds, *but for the greatest sin of refusing to accept the truth of who Jesus is.*

A further warning from Jesus brings all the others into the present tense. Speaking of the need to believe in him, he added, *...whoever does not believe is condemned already, because he has not believed in the name of the only Son of God* (John 3:18).

These warnings are dire and dreadful, and ignoring them is spiritual suicide. They also illustrate something of God's great love in sending his Son to alert us to their danger and to provide for us the only possible escape.

Thirdly, *all his promises are true*. God makes hundreds of *precious and very great promises* (2 Peter 1:4) in the Bible, many of them directly from the lips of Jesus. Speaking to those who were shackled by religious rules and regulations, vainly hoping that observing these would make them right with God, he promised, *Come to me, all who labour and are heavy laden, and I will give you rest* (Matthew 11:28). So today, Jesus promises to anyone who genuinely turns from leaning on religion or personal moral performance and trusts only in him peace of heart and mind and an assurance that they have been forgiven.

Another promise underlines this: *Whoever hears my word and believes him who sent me **has** eternal life. He does not come into judgement, but **has passed** from death to life* (John 5:24). I have emphasized the verbs to underline their value. Eternal life for the Christian is something that begins not after death but at the moment he puts his trust in Jesus Christ. On the final Day of Judgement, condemnation is impossible for the Christian, because Jesus has already paid in full the penalty the believer deserves. Nor does the Christian need to fear the dreadful 'death' of eternal punishment brought about by sin, as his Saviour has already endured it on his behalf.

Jesus made another promise that relates directly to the subject of this booklet: *I am the resurrection and the life. Whoever believes in me, though he die, yet shall he live* (John 11:25). For countless people death is a terrifying prospect, filled with fear of the unknown or fear of meeting God. At the height of his career, and with a well-earned reputation for courage and daring, the British racing driver Stirling Moss told a newspaper reporter, *I am frightened of death. I know it means going to meet one's Maker, and one shouldn't be afraid of that, but I am.* For the person who trusts in Jesus Christ for salvation there is no such fear. In a Bible passage we looked at earlier, Paul spelled out what followed if Jesus has not risen from the dead, then added, *But in fact Christ has been raised from the dead, the firstfruits of those who have fallen asleep* (1 Corinthians 15:20). Paul's readers would have been familiar with the idea of 'firstfruits'. These were the first crops to ripen and were gathered in and offered to God in thanksgiving (see Deuteronomy 26:1-19). They also represented all the crops that were to follow and Paul says that Jesus had represented those for whom he died, not only in his death, *but also in his resurrection.* As C. S. Lewis wrote, *He has forced open a door that had been closed since the death of the first man* — and he did so on behalf of all who put their trust in him. His resurrection guarantees the resurrection of everyone in whose place he died.

Paul then underlined his illustration: *For as by a man came death, by a man has come also the resurrection of the dead. For as in Adam all die, so also in Christ shall all be made alive* (1 Corinthians 15:21-22). As we have already seen, Adam was the representative head of the entire human race. The name 'Adam' literally means 'mankind'. All mankind existed in him and when he sinned all mankind sinned. This explains why, as his descendants, we are all heirs, not only to deterioration and disease, but to both physical and spiritual death.

Now comes the good news for those who put their trust in Jesus Christ! Because he is their representative head, *they share in all that he accomplished.* Just as there is a direct relationship between the death of Adam and the death of his descendants, so there is one between the resurrection of Jesus and the resurrection of those in whose place he died. He conquered death; so will they. He ascended into heaven; so will they. The person who trusts in Jesus Christ is as certain to spend eternity in heaven as is Jesus himself. The Bible goes even further and says that in heaven those who have put their trust in Jesus *shall be like him* (1 John 3:2). It is a breathtaking prospect! Just as the first Adam brought all the miseries of eternal death upon everyone in the human race, so Jesus — the Bible calls him 'the last Adam' (1 Corinthians 15:45) — brings all the glories of eternal life to everyone who trusts in him.

There is no greater promise in the entire Bible!

Your call

God's promises are often linked to commands. They are not like a vague 'take it or leave it' offer. One example speaks for many others. God promises, *You will seek me and find me when you seek me with all your heart* (Jeremiah 29:13, NIV) — but he also gives this clear command: *Seek the Lord while he may be found; call upon him while he is near* (Isaiah 55:6). What is your response? To ignore his promise and disobey his command is to flash your fist in God's face and to seal your appalling fate for ever. To believe his promise and obey his command is to discover for yourself that *the free gift of God is eternal life in Christ Jesus our Lord* (Romans 6:23).

Then seek him *now*, confess your sin and your need of salvation, and ask him to enable you to turn from sin and to put your trust in Jesus Christ, the one who is *the true God and eternal life* (1 John 5:20).